Beyond Speedcubing

A Decade of Pursuing Dreams

CHINMAY PRABHU

With the blessings of God and the unwavering support of my parents, I dedicate this book to all the dreamers and fighters out there. This is for everyone who dares to chase their passions, who perseveres in the face of adversity, and who never gives up despite the odds.

Thank you to every single person who has been a part of my decade-long journey, your encouragement, love, and belief have been my greatest strengths.

Contents

Preface

In early 2015, I stumbled upon a fascinating sport that would profoundly shape my life: speedcubing. What began as a curious interest in solving colorful cube puzzles quickly grew into a passionate pursuit of excellence, pushing me to redefine my own limits. Along the way, I discovered the immense power of blending different interests, merging speedcubing with other sports to achieve world records and defy expectations.

This book is more than just my story, it's an invitation for you to join me on a journey of exploration and personal growth. Whether you're contemplating picking up a new hobby, chasing after a challenging goal, or nurturing a dream that's been quietly calling to you, now is the perfect time to take that brave first step forward. Embrace the excitement of learning something new or mastering a skill that has always intrigued you. It's through these passionate pursuits that we discover what truly brings us joy and purpose in life.As you delve into these pages, my hope is that my experiences will ignite a spark within you to courageously pursue your own aspirations, to push beyond the obstacles, and to uncover the extraordinary potential that lies within each of us. This book chronicles a journey of resilience, of setbacks turned into triumphs, and of the profound fulfillment found in relentlessly pursuing what sets your soul on fire.

Welcome to a journey where every twist of the cube mirrors the twists and turns of our own personal journeys.

Sincerely,

Chinmay Prabhu

Acknowledgments

First and foremost, I would like to extend my deepest gratitude to the entire team of Cubenama. Your unwavering support and dedication over the years have been instrumental in my journey of setting records. Your commitment and enthusiasm have been a cornerstone of my success.

A special thank you to Farza, whose encouragement and motivation in season 5 of Buildspace inspired me to embark on new challenges and expand my horizons. Your guidance has been invaluable.

I am profoundly grateful to Prince Trivedi for his unconditional support throughout this journey. Your belief in me and your constant encouragement have been a source of strength and inspiration.

Lastly, my heartfelt thanks to Clarence Johnson for designing the cover of this book. Your artistic vision and creativity have brought this project to life, and without your contribution, this book would not have achieved its full potential.

To all of you, I am eternally grateful. Thank you for being an integral part of this journey.

Introduction

Picture this: a 23-year-old standing at the edge of an aircraft, 13,000 feet above the ground. His heart pounds, and adrenaline courses through his veins. In his hands, he holds a colorful puzzle. His mission? To solve it while falling towards the earth at high speed.

Sounds crazy, right? Well, that's me. I'm the guy who turned a love for puzzles into a wild adventure that took me from the streets of Mumbai to the skies of Thailand.

But how did I get here? How does someone go from being a regular college student, navigating the chaotic buses and trains of Mumbai, to a holder of several Guinness World Record titles, solving puzzles underwater and in freefall? The answer lies in a combination of passion, perseverance, and perhaps a touch of pleasant madness.

It's a tale of transformation, of pushing boundaries not just in the physical world, but in the realm of what we believe is possible. It's about finding joy in the most unexpected places and turning setbacks into comebacks. From the moment I picked up my first puzzle, to the heart-stopping seconds of my bubble record attempt, every twist and turn has shaped who I am today.

As you flip through these pages, you'll join me on a journey filled with laughter, tears, triumph, and more than a few puzzling moments.

So, buckle up and get ready for a ride that defies gravity and logic. Whether you're a fellow puzzle enthusiast, an aspiring record-breaker, or just someone looking for a bit of inspiration, I hope my story reminds you that with passion, determination, and a touch of madness, anything is possible.

CHAPTER ONE

DESTINY

Growing up, I was never really into cubing. To be honest, I didn't even know the sport existed. Sure, I saw those colorful cube puzzles in almost every other store, but I never felt the urge to pick one up and see what all the fuss was about. My parents, on the other hand, were always encouraging me to push my boundaries and learn something new each summer vacation. My mom, especially, had this incredible drive to keep me engaged and active. She would sign me up for swimming lessons, dance classes, skating, and a ton of other activities. It seemed like she always wanted me to stay busy, to explore the world around me, and to discover my passions. She believed in the importance of a well-rounded upbringing, and she made sure I had every opportunity to find out what I loved.

Out of all the activities I took up, swimming quickly became my favorite. There was something magical about being in the water that made me feel truly free. The way the water supported my body, the rhythm of my strokes, and the feeling of gliding through the pool all combined to create a sense of liberation unlike anything else I had experienced. I loved learning new techniques and challenging myself to hold my breath longer, striving to swim without having to come up for air too often. Each time I glided through the water, it felt like I was discovering a new part of myself, testing my limits, and experiencing a profound sense of liberation. Swimming wasn't just an activity; it was my escape, my way of embracing the boundless freedom the water offered.

When summer vacations came to an end, I would transition back to the school's curriculum and shift my focus to my studies. As the end of my school days approached, the pressure to excel became more intense, especially with the looming board exams. The pressure to score well was immense, and it seemed to touch every aspect of my life. Teachers, parents, and even friends constantly reminded me of the importance of these exams. It felt like a make-or-break moment that would define my future.

Oddly enough, I found it difficult to study during the day. The world outside felt too noisy, too full of distractions. The daytime was full of sounds and activities that pulled my attention in a million different directions. But the nights—oh, the nights were entirely different. When the sun dipped below the horizon and the world grew still, a serene silence would blanket everything. It was in this quiet that I found my perfect study environment.

I have always enjoyed working and studying in silence. There's something about the stillness of the night that sharpens my focus and calms my mind. In those silent hours, I could immerse myself fully in my books, absorbing information with a clarity that seemed impossible during the day. The world seemed to pause, allowing me to delve deeply into my studies without interruption. Those quiet, nocturnal study sessions became my sanctuary, a time when I could connect with my thoughts and prepare for the challenges ahead.

The exams went well, and I managed to score a decent percentage, enough to get me into the Science stream. The relief of seeing my results was immense, and I felt a sense of accomplishment wash over me. With the results in hand, I carefully chose the college I wanted to apply to, not realizing then that this place would be the starting point of my speedcubing destiny. I was thrilled when I received my admission letter, and even more excited to step into a new chapter of my life.

The prospect of college life filled me with anticipation and a touch of nervousness.

College brought a whirlwind of experiences and new friendships. There was something special about the group of friends I made there. They had an energy, a passion for life, that was contagious. I found myself drawn to them, eager to spend time with them, and ready to share in their adventures. Our conversations were lively, our laughter frequent, and our bond quickly grew strong.

Among these new friends was someone who introduced me to the fascinating world of speedcubing. At first, I was skeptical. How could a simple cube puzzle be so captivating? But their enthusiasm was infectious, and soon enough, I found myself picking up a cube and giving it a try. Initially, I tried solving the puzzle by making random twists and turns, but it wasn't taking me anywhere. I then realized that it wasn't just simple logic but rather some algorithms to follow along with logic. I tried looking on the internet and to my surprise there were many tutorials. The problem was, most of them had different ways to approach solving the puzzle. If I messed up one single move, it meant I had to start right from the beginning, and if I decided to watch a different video, the approach would change, making it more confusing. I decided to stick to one video tutorial and kept trying for multiple days and soon after, I was able to crack the puzzle. It didn't take long for me to get hooked. The more I practiced, the more intrigued I became by the challenge and the satisfaction of solving the cube.

This group of friends was different from any I'd had before. They challenged me, supported me, and pushed me to explore new interests. With their encouragement, I began to take speedcubing seriously. We would spend hours practicing, sharing tips, and celebrating each other's progress. Our shared passion for speedcubing created a bond that was both unique and incredibly rewarding.

Looking back, I realize that this college, and these friends, were pivotal in shaping my journey. They helped me discover a passion I never knew I had and taught me the value of persistence and community. The lessons I learned and the friendships I made during this time remain some of the most cherished memories of my life.

My mother's push for me to stay active and engaged as a child, my discovery of swimming as a passion, and my night-time study habits all played a role in who I became. But it was the new experiences and friendships in college that truly shaped my path. They led me to speedcubing, a passion that I might never have discovered on my own. And through speedcubing, I learned the importance of perseverance, the joy of shared interests, and the value of a supportive community.

Reflecting on my own journey, I can't help but wonder about the childhood experiences that shape each of us in unique ways. What activities or passions ignited your spirit as a child? Was it a particular sport, a creative hobby, or perhaps the quiet moments of self-discovery in your own sanctuary? Think back to those early days when the world seemed vast and full of possibilities. Remember the people who encouraged you, the friends who joined you on adventures, and the simple joys that filled your days. How did those moments influence the person you have become today? As we grow older, it's easy to forget the impact of our formative years, but they often hold the key to understanding our deepest passions and aspirations. Take a moment to revisit those memories, and let them remind you of the dreams that once sparked your imagination.

CHAPTER TWO

CURIOSITY

Once I figured out how to solve the colorful cube puzzle, my curiosity was on peak, and I was eager to learn more. Delving into the vast resources of the internet, I discovered an entire universe of puzzles, each with different shapes, sizes, and complexities.

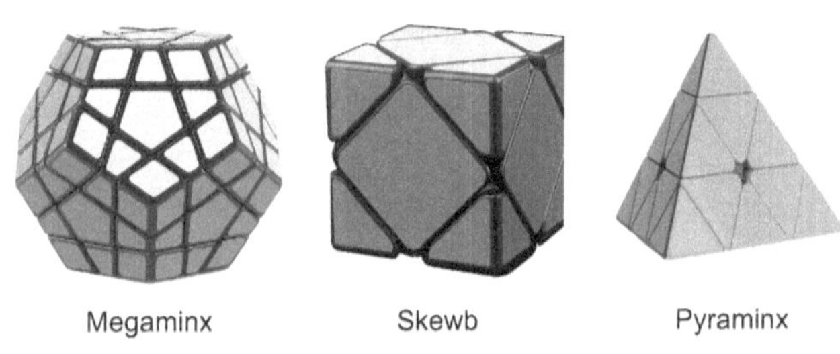

Megaminx   Skewb   Pyraminx

The variety was staggering and immensely exciting. Every week, I would learn how to solve a new puzzle and then eagerly request my dad to buy me another one. This became a regular routine until, one day, our home was overflowing with nearly a hundred puzzles. Every corner, shelf, and the table was occupied by these fascinating puzzles. Eventually, it got to the point where I didn't know where to keep them all. Our house had transformed into a huge puzzle wonderland.

My passion for these puzzles wasn't limited to solving them by hand. I pushed my boundaries further by learning to solve them with my feet. The challenge and novelty of these different methods only deepened my love for speedcubing. It became more than just a hobby—it became my passion, my obsession. Every single day, I practiced diligently, not to compare myself with others but to compete against my own previous times. I was driven by a desire to be a better version of myself each day, to continually improve my skills and technique.

Wherever I went, my cube went with me. Whether I was traveling or sitting through those inevitably dull college lectures, I would always be fidgeting with my cube. The tactile feedback and the mental challenge provided a unique form of comfort and stimulation.

In retrospect, I had tried many activities before discovering speedcubing, but none captivated me as this did. Swimming, dance, skating—they all required specific environments, equipment, or partners. Speedcubing, on the other hand, demanded nothing but the puzzle itself. It was a perfect blend of mental and physical challenge, and it provided an endless source of fun and fulfillment. The more I practiced, the more I realized that this was not just a passing interest but a true passion that brought immense joy and satisfaction into my life.

As I was practicing speedcubing with my friends one afternoon, one of them casually mentioned that there were upcoming competitions in Mumbai. "Maybe we should participate", he suggested with a spark of excitement in his eyes. I was taken aback. Competitions? For speedcubing? Until that moment, I had no idea such events even existed. I had assumed that speedcubing was just a fun hobby for a niche group of enthusiasts.

In my mind, I envisioned a small gathering of perhaps 10 to 15 people, mostly kids, casually solving their cubes while their parents watched. The idea of competing was thrilling. I imagined myself stepping into the competition room and blowing everyone away with my newfound skills, leaving the crowd in awe. Eager to take on this new challenge, I decided to register for the competition. After some deliberation, I signed up for two categories: the regular 3x3 cube and the pyraminx, a pyramid-shaped puzzle that had recently piqued my interest.

The days leading up to the competition were filled with a mix of anticipation and nervousness. I practiced relentlessly, honing my techniques and memorizing algorithms until they became second nature. My friends and I would gather every day, timing each other's solves and sharing tips to improve our speed and accuracy. We bonded over our shared interest, and our excitement grew every day.

The event was held in Juhu, Mumbai, a bustling area known for its beach and vibrant atmosphere. As I arrived at the venue, a wave of anxiety washed over me. I had anticipated a modest turnout, maybe 10 or 15 kids like me, nervously clutching their cubes. Instead, I found myself among 189 participants, a veritable sea of competitors all buzzing with excitement and anticipation. I had just begun my journey into speedcubing, and suddenly, I was thrust into the deep end of the pool.

The competition room was filled with the sounds of cubes clicking, people chatting, and the occasional cheer or groan as a solve was completed. My heart raced as I tried to steady my nerves. Soon enough, my name was called, and I made my way to the designated chair, ready for my first official Pyraminx solve. The moment was surreal. I sat down, took a deep breath, and said, "I'm ready." The covered box in front of me was lifted, revealing the scrambled Pyraminx. The observation stopwatch began ticking, and I examined the puzzle, my mind racing to figure out the best starting point.

I placed the puzzle back down and positioned my hands on the timer, waiting for the light on the timer to turn green. When it did, I picked up the Pyraminx and started turning it swiftly, my fingers moving instinctively through the motions I had practiced countless times. But something was different. My movements felt slower, my thoughts more jumbled. After what felt like an eternity but was only a few seconds, I completed the solve and slammed the puzzle down. The timer read 20.36 seconds.

I stared at the time in disbelief. During practice, I had been much faster, consistently solving the Pyraminx in well under 20 seconds. But here, in the heat of competition, my nerves had gotten the better of me. The disappointment was sharp, but so was the realization that this was just the beginning. I had taken the first step into the competitive world of speedcubing, and despite the nerves and the unexpected pressure, I had completed my first official solve.

As I walked back to my seat, I couldn't help but reflect on the experience. The competition was more intense than I had imagined, but it also ignited a fire within me. I was determined to improve, to conquer my nerves, and to become faster. That day in Juhu, amidst other cubers, I found not only a challenge but also a community and a sense of purpose. The journey had begun, and I was ready to embrace it, one solve at a time.

As the competition continued, I found myself increasingly immersed in the atmosphere. Watching other participants, both veterans and newcomers like myself, was inspiring. Each solve was a display of skill, speed, and intense focus. I realized that I wasn't just competing against the clock; I was part of a vibrant community where everyone shared the same passion. There was a strong feeling of togetherness, and it was reassuring to know that I wasn't alone in my journey. Conversations flowed easily between rounds, with competitors exchanging tips, discussing techniques, and even sharing stories of their cubing adventures. I felt a deep connection with these people who, just like me, found joy in the colorful, twisting puzzles.

The rest of the day passed in a blur of excitement and learning. I participated in the 3x3 cube category as well, managing to improve my times with each successive attempt. The initial nerves had given way to a calm focus, and I began to enjoy the competition for what it was—a celebration of our shared passion. As I watched the more experienced cubers perform mind-boggling solves in mere seconds, I was filled with admiration and a renewed determination to reach their level one day. The event concluded with an award ceremony, and though I didn't take home any trophies, I left with something far more valuable: a clear vision of what I wanted to achieve and the steps I needed to take to get there.

Returning home that evening, I couldn't stop thinking about the competition and the people I had met. My mind buzzed with ideas and strategies for improving my speed and efficiency. I set up a more structured practice schedule, incorporating the tips and techniques I had learned from my fellow competitors. My friends and I continued to meet regularly, pushing each other to new heights and celebrating our progress. The experience in Juhu, Mumbai had ignited a fire within me, and I was more motivated than ever to pursue my passion for speedcubing. The journey ahead promised to be challenging, but I embraced it with enthusiasm and optimism, knowing that every twist and turn would bring me closer to my goals.

March of 2016 marked a thrilling new chapter in my journey. I participated in the Indian Nationals 2016 in New Delhi, the biggest competition I'd ever attended. Legends of the sport would be there, and I felt a mix of excitement and nervousness. I traveled with friends from the speedcubing community, though my excitement extended beyond the competition—I was eager to explore New Delhi, try local food, and soak in the new experiences.

One of the days brought a unique challenge: I was set to compete in an event for the first time—solving a cube using only my feet. This was an official event back in 2016. The experience was both fun and frustrating. I knew exactly what moves to make, but my feet struggled to grip the cube, turning the process into a bit of a mess. It took me 6 minutes and 28 seconds to solve the puzzle. Despite the challenges, I felt a surge of pride in completing it.

CHAPTER THREE

MANIFESTATION

When I started participating in numerous speedcubing competitions, my skills began to sharpen, and I saw significant progress. Each event brought new challenges, new strategies, and a deeper appreciation for the intricacies of speedcubing. It was during one of these competitions that I encountered something truly inspiring—a record attempt for the Limca Book of Records title. Until that moment, I had been unaware of such a Book of Records, but witnessing the attempt was an eye-opening experience.

The atmosphere was electric, with spectators on the edge of their seats and competitors displaying a mix of nerves and excitement. The record attempt involved solving the most number of puzzles in an incredibly short amount of time by a team, and the precision and speed of the solver were nothing short of mesmerizing. Watching the attempt unfold was thrilling. The concentration, the deft movements, and the ultimate triumph of setting a new record were captivating. It was a performance that combined skill, practice, and an indomitable spirit.

After the competition, I couldn't shake the excitement I felt from witnessing the record attempt. As soon as I got home, I dove into researching more about the Book of Records. I spent hours surfing the internet, delving into its history and the variety of records it celebrated. I discovered that the Limca Book of Records, honors remarkable achievements across a multitude of disciplines. It shines a spotlight on extraordinary feats performed by ordinary people, showcasing the incredible potential of human endeavor.

The more I learned, the more fascinated I became. I read about individuals who had set records in everything from marathon running to unique culinary creations. Each story was a testament to human ingenuity and determination. I was particularly drawn to the records related to puzzles and mental challenges, finding kindred spirits in those who shared my passion for solving the seemingly unsolvable.

The idea of attempting a record began to take root in my mind. It seemed like the perfect next step in my speedcubing journey, a new challenge to push my limits and test my abilities. The stories I read were not just about setting records; they were about pushing boundaries, overcoming obstacles, and achieving the extraordinary. They inspired me to envision my own name among those who had accomplished the remarkable.

As I continued to compete and improve, the dream of setting a record became a driving force, a manifestation of my dedication. It wasn't just about the recognition; it was about the journey—the countless hours of practice, the strategies developed, the mistakes learned from, and the ultimate satisfaction of achieving a goal that once seemed impossible. The Book of Records represented a new horizon, a chance to elevate my passion for speedcubing to new heights and inspire others with my story.

This newfound ambition infused my training with a renewed sense of purpose. Every solve, every practice session, became a step towards a larger goal. I was no longer just competing against others or even myself; I was preparing to make my mark on the national stage, to join the ranks of those who had dared to achieve the exceptional.

There was an existing record for solving the mirror cube blindfolded that caught my attention. I already knew how to solve the mirror cube, but doing it blindfolded seemed like a huge challenge. Unlike the standard cube puzzle, where you rely on colors, the mirror cube's pieces are all the same color but different shapes. This means you have to feel the pieces and understand where each one needs to go just by touch.

Determined to break the record, I practiced every day for about four months. Each day, I would close my eyes and rely solely on my sense of touch, slowly but surely getting better at it. Finally, I was ready to take on the national record.

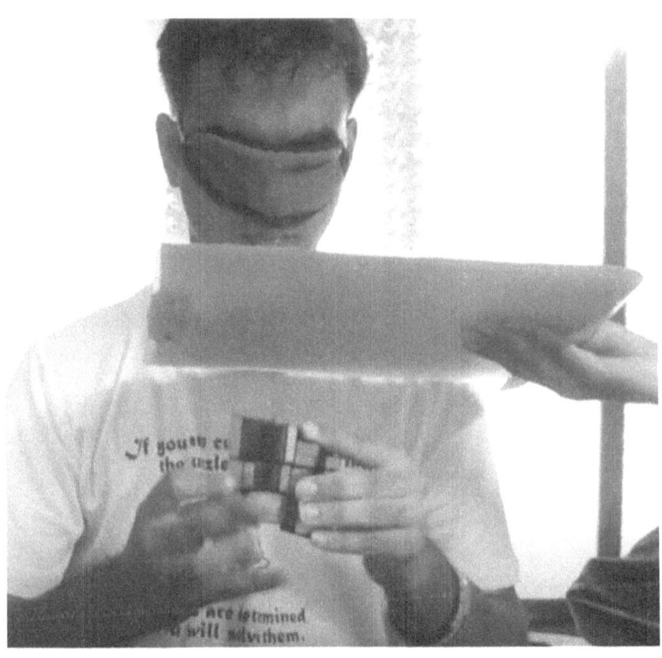

The attempt was one of the most stressful experiences of my life, but the hard work paid off. I successfully broke the record, and the moment it was confirmed, I was over the moon with excitement.

When the certificate arrived, my heart was racing as I opened the package. Seeing the certificate with "National Record" and my name on it was a surreal moment. I felt an overwhelming sense of pride and joy. Like any other teenager, I immediately wanted to share my achievement with the world. I posted it on social media, and soon, comments started flooding in from friends and family. Everyone was so happy for me, and some even commented, "A World Record next!"

While I appreciated the support, those comments also made me feel a bit overwhelmed. Setting a national record was one thing, but a World Record? That seemed impossible. The pressure of those expectations weighed on me, but it also planted a seed of possibility in my mind.

CHAPTER FOUR

NOSTALGIA

It was early 2018 when I decided to attempt a World Record with a unique twist. I had always loved swimming during my school days, and speedcubing had become my new passion. One day, an idea struck me: why not combine the two? But how? I pondered this question for days until it finally hit me—I could try to solve the most pyramid-shaped puzzles in one breath while sitting underwater.

After some research, I discovered that no one had attempted this record before for solving Pyraminx puzzles underwater in a single breath. It seemed like the perfect opportunity to set a new record. I thought even solving just one or two puzzles would make me a world record holder. Excitedly, I sent my idea ahead and soon received a set of instructions or rather guidelines to follow for the attempt to be considered successful. To my surprise, they also set a target for me: I had to solve a minimum of four puzzles. That was when I realized that setting a record was never meant to be easy; it required pushing beyond the ordinary. Four puzzles? That didn't seem too tough, I thought. I needed to start practicing immediately.

The first step was to find a place where I could practice. I needed a swimming pool that would allow me to bring my puzzles into the water. So, I began cold-calling every sports arena and swimming facility nearby. To my dismay, nobody would allow me to go into the pool with an object like a cube. It made no sense to me—how could a small puzzle be an obstruction? Undeterred, I kept calling, visiting multiple places, and explaining my idea, only to be met with repeated denials. Each rejection chipped away at my hope. If given a chance, I might or might not succeed, but not getting a chance at all meant I was guaranteed to fail. With each passing day, my optimism dwindled.

Over 20 days of the month went by with no success. Just like every other day, I visited yet another place to pitch my idea. To my surprise, they were interested in helping me out. It was a Sports Club. I couldn't believe it. Words failed me as I tried to explain my vision. They listened attentively and finally agreed to let me practice under one condition: I could only use the pool during non-operational hours, when it was closed to their members.

I was more than okay with it. At this point, I would have agreed to any condition just to see this happen. All I was asking was for a chance. Practicing during non-operational hours meant I would have to skip two of my college lectures daily to reach the pool on time. But I was determined. The dream of setting a world record fueled my resolve, and I was willing to make any sacrifice necessary.

Once I agreed to their condition, they told me I could start practicing the very next day. I went home, my mind buzzing with excitement and a bit of nervousness. I started packing my bag, carefully folding my swimwear, and gathering all the essentials I would need. This was it—the first real step toward achieving my dream. As I lay in bed that night, my thoughts raced. I couldn't sleep at all, my mind filled with visions of the pool and what lay ahead.

The next morning, I was up before the alarm went off. I headed to my college to attend all the lectures in the morning. I kept glancing at the clock, my anticipation growing with each passing minute. I explained the situation to my professors and they did not seem to have a problem with me skipping the class as long as I would complete their assignments on time. When it was finally time, I grabbed my bag and rushed out of the class, my heart pounding like I was running away from a monster. The reason for my haste was clear: I had a very limited window to practice while the pool was non-operational, and I couldn't afford to waste a single minute. A friend from my class who was heading out too for his internship, offered me a ride.

When I arrived at the location, I stepped into the changing room, I felt a surge of energy. I quickly changed into my swimming gear, my hands almost trembling with anticipation. As I opened the main door of the locker room and stepped out, there it was: a gigantic Olympic pool, stretching out before me like a shimmering blue expanse. It looked even more beautiful than I remembered, the water calm and inviting under the soft lighting. This was the same pool where I had spent countless hours practicing as a child, honing my skills and dreaming of the future.

Entering that familiar space after so many years felt incredibly nostalgic, filled with a profound sense of nostalgia. Memories of my younger self, splashing around and striving to improve, came flooding back. I took a deep breath, the scent of chlorine bringing a comforting sense of familiarity. Standing there, I felt a profound connection to my past and a renewed determination for the future.

I walked to the edge of the pool, the water gently lapping against the sides. Taking a moment to absorb the scene, I realized this was more than just a practice session. It was a homecoming, a return to the place where my dreams first took shape. With a mixture of reverence and excitement, I took my first step into the water, feeling the cool embrace of the pool around me. It was time to begin again.

CHAPTER FIVE

ROUTINE

I went in confidently, determined to challenge myself. I brought a few pyramid-shaped puzzles along, eager to see how many I could solve. However, when I tried holding my breath while solving the puzzles, I was shocked by how difficult it was. What I had assumed would be easy turned out to be a daunting task. I couldn't hold my breath for even ten seconds, and trying to solve the puzzles simultaneously was nearly impossible. My hands kept moving, and my mind refused to stay quiet, rapidly consuming all the oxygen I was holding.

I decided to give it another try, but the result was the same. As I struggled, doubt began to creep in. Had I made a mistake by taking on this challenge? Was my confidence, bolstered by my national record, merely overconfidence? The questions echoed in my mind, leaving me to reconsider my approach and the limits of my abilities.

I didn't know what to say. I kept trying over and over, but it wasn't helping. It felt like I'd already lost on day one of my practice. When I got back home, my parents were curious to know how the practice had gone. Their questions annoyed me so much that I switched off the television and retreated to my room. I was simply unhappy with myself, feeling like I had no control over the practice whatsoever. It was only the first day, but I knew my overconfidence had let me down.

Desperate for answers, I started watching videos on the internet that suggested techniques for holding your breath longer. Most of them had straightforward advice: concentrate on holding your breath, make no body movements, and try not to think about anything. Stay as calm as possible. But this clearly wasn't helping. What I was trying to achieve wasn't going to happen by staying calm, or so I thought.

Day two started with a knot of anxiety in my stomach. I was so nervous that I skipped my classes, pretending to be sick. I wasn't sick; I was just terrified of failing again. When the time came, I packed my bag and headed straight to my practice session. This time, I left the pyramid-shaped puzzles behind. My only goal was to hold my breath for as long as possible.

I sat beside the pool, looking up at the bright, sunny sky, and prayed for strength. I needed to be a better version of myself today. Taking a few deep breaths, I set a stopwatch by the pool, took one final deep breath, and then closed my nose with my index fingers. In my mind, I counted down: 3, 2, 1. With all my might, I plunged into the water. Slowly, I released my fingers from my nose and tried to stay underwater as long as I could.

As the seconds ticked by, my head started to ache, but I pushed through the discomfort. I wasn't giving up so easily this time. Finally, when I couldn't take it any longer, I surfaced and stopped the stopwatch, gasping for air. My head was buzzing with the rush of oxygen. The timer showed 15 seconds.

I wasn't entirely happy, but I felt a glimmer of satisfaction. I had pushed my limits today. On day one, I hadn't kept track of how long I stayed underwater, but I was sure today had been longer. It wasn't easy, but I knew there was some progress. Practice sessions like this became a routine.

As days went by, not every practice session was better than the last, but I kept pushing myself. It wasn't just about improving my performance; it was about committing to practice every single day. I had one rule: no skipping practice, no matter what. I didn't want overconfidence to trip me up again.

After about twenty-five days of diligent practice, I could hold my breath underwater for around fifty seconds. This was a significant achievement, but it only applied to breath holding without any distractions. Knowing I needed to tackle the real challenge, I began incorporating puzzles into my underwater sessions.

As I shifted my focus to solving puzzles underwater, my breath-holding time initially decreased. Concentrating on the puzzles made it harder to stay submerged for as long. However, this time I was able to solve the puzzles completely, marking real progress. My journey was far from over, but I was beginning to see the fruits of my relentless practice and dedication.

The days kept passing and by now I was solving 4 puzzles straight. I knew I was ready to set the world record. But now seeing the way I was progressing now I wanted to solve even more. I did not just want to stop at the 4 puzzle mark. I kept practicing even harder now. Not everyday but sometimes practicing with nobody at the pool side made me feel less motivated. After weeks of practice, the guard now allowed me to even take one of my friends along with me for the practice.

This friend was the same guy who dropped me at the place on day 1 of practice while heading to his internship.

He would join me almost every other week, tracking my progress and keeping me motivated. I felt so grateful to have a friend like him. With his support, I kept practicing relentlessly, constantly pushing my limits. Some days, my dad would show up at the practice site just to see how I was doing. The pride in his eyes was unmistakable, and it fueled my determination even more.

The time had come to make my country proud. After weeks of grueling practice, I was ready to attempt setting a world record. By this time, Cubenama was actively organizing competitions in Mumbai and had their own cube store as well. I too was a part of team Cubenama. I knew I couldn't do it alone; I needed my team to set this World Record title. I reached out to my friends from Cubenama. As soon as they heard what I was preparing for, they were all in. We planned a mock session for Saturday morning and the record attempt for Sunday.

On Friday night, my friends gathered at my apartment. We discussed the event flow, how everything would happen, how we would collect evidence, and, most importantly, we cleaned all the puzzles. We went over the setup for the cameras and decided where the desks for the witnesses, scramblers, and timekeepers would be placed. We left no stone unturned. I printed all the required documents and packed them in a folder.

The next morning, we headed to the site of the attempt. I walked through the premises with my college friend, my dad, and the Cubenama team. As we approached the lobby, we were greeted by a huge banner detailing the record attempt. I hadn't seen it before; it was a surprise from the club where I had been practicing. My dad was so happy, he immediately stood next to the banner, wanting a picture.

Seeing the banner and the excitement in everyone's eyes filled me with a mixture of pride and anticipation. This was it. All the hard work, all the hours of practice, had led to this moment. With my team by my side and the support of my family and friends, I felt ready to take on the challenge and make history.

We walked to the pool site, and everyone immediately sprang into action. Some of my friends coordinated with the staff to finalize the timings for the next day, while others tested the cameras and checked if we needed anything additional for the attempt. Meanwhile, I began my warm-up, trying to hold my breath for longer. My warm-up usually took no more than fifteen minutes. I was ready for the mock attempt.

Most of those present were witnessing this process for the first time. Taking a deep breath, I submerged myself underwater. I sat calmly and began solving puzzles one after the other. I had been advised not to push my limits today to avoid exhaustion. Despite this, I gave it my best shot and managed to solve seven pyramid-shaped puzzles. After two more mock attempts, I was told to step out of the water.

I then joined my team to review the camera angles and planned filming positions. Everything looked good to me, and I felt a wave of excitement for the next day. The preparation, the coordination, and the practice had all led up to this moment.

The anticipation of attempting a World Record the next day was starting to sink in. Up until now, my practice sessions had gone well, but I couldn't shake the hope that everything would go smoothly when it really counted. The mix of excitement and fear made it hard to focus on anything else.

CHAPTER SIX

SETBACK

On July 22nd, 2018, I was all geared up for the big attempt. Sitting in the locker room, my anxiety started to build. I had always practiced alone in the pool, but now, with so many eyes on me, the pressure was intense. I got dressed and stepped out of the locker room. People lined the sides of the pool, cheering me on for my attempt.

I entered the pool, full of hope to beat the target of solving four pyramid-shaped puzzles underwater and aiming to go even higher. The guidelines for the attempt were announced while the witnesses, timekeepers, and guests listened attentively. I took a deep breath, closed my nose with my fingers, and in my mind, I counted down: 3, 2, 1, Go! I submerged myself underwater.

Releasing my hands from my nose, I grabbed the first puzzle and started solving it as quickly as I could. Once I solved it, I released the puzzle and grabbed another scrambled one. This process repeated over and over. I didn't keep track of how many puzzles I was solving; I just kept going until I was extremely out of breath. When I finally couldn't hold my breath any longer, I surfaced, gasping for air. The audience erupted in applause and cheers. I had solved nine puzzles in a single breath. It felt unreal and magical.

Afterward, all the formalities were completed and evidence was sent. Every day, I checked my email, eagerly waiting for the news I wanted to hear.

Finally, one day, an email popped up. I opened it, feeling happy and excited, but as I read the contents, my heart sank. The attempt had been disqualified. The email explained that I had failed to follow one of the many guidelines, resulting in the disqualification of my record attempt.

The disappointment was overwhelming. After all the preparation and the excitement of the attempt, it was a crushing blow to find out that a small mistake had cost me the record. But even in that moment of setback, I knew that I had to keep pushing forward and learn from the experience.

Since the email arrived about 45 days after my attempt, I knew I had to practice again if I wanted another shot at the record. The day after receiving the disheartening news, I went back to the managing authorities of the sports club after a week and asked if I could practice for a few weeks to prepare for another attempt. I told them I accepted that there had been an oversight, but I wouldn't let that stop me from achieving my goal. They saw the determination in my eyes and trusted me. Not only did I get permission, but the staff was more supportive this time. They knew how much this meant to me.

I began my practice routine all over again. It took several more weeks this time because it was impossible to attempt the record during the monsoon season. Despite the rain, I never stopped practicing. I gave it everything I had, rain or shine.

Once I felt ready, I planned to attempt the record on December 9th, 2018. Same preparations had begun. Sitting in the locker room before the attempt, I felt the same mix of excitement and nerves as before. This time, the pressure was even more intense. Not only did I have to follow all the guidelines perfectly, but I also didn't want to solve fewer than nine puzzles, the number I achieved in my first attempt. I didn't want anyone to dismiss my first attempt at solving nine puzzles as mere luck. I could feel the rise of anticipation within me as the moment approached.

I entered the pool, all geared up, with an even larger audience to witness it live. Taking a deep breath, I submerged myself underwater. I focused on solving the puzzles one after the other, giving it my all.

When I finally came up for air, gasping and exhausted, I had no idea how many puzzles I had managed to solve. The pressure of keeping track had been too distracting. As I broke the surface, I heard the news: I had successfully solved nine pyramid-shaped puzzles in just 1 minute and 48 seconds.

I sent the evidence ahead, and nearly 90 days later, I received an email stating that the record had been verified. I was now a Guinness World Record Title Holder. The moment felt unreal. My heartbeat was racing as I opened the package containing the certificate. This time, the feeling was different from when I received the national record certificate. Seeing my name on the certificate stating it was a national record made me happy, but seeing "India" on the World Record certificate made me even prouder. My name was secondary to the pride I felt for representing my country.

Holding that certificate in my hands, I realized how much the journey had transformed me. It wasn't just about breaking a record anymore; it was about perseverance, learning from mistakes, and rising above challenges. The support from the community, the countless hours of practice, and the unwavering belief in my goal all culminated in that single, magical moment. It was a testament to the power of resilience and determination, and it filled me with an overwhelming sense of accomplishment and gratitude.

The fire was now ignited within me. Achieving this record had only fueled my ambition, and I was more determined than ever to set even more records. With renewed confidence and the taste of success still fresh, I knew this was just the beginning. I started planning my next challenges, eager to push my limits further and continue making my mark.

CHAPTER SEVEN

RHYTHM

In 2018, I set myself a unique challenge: to participate in a marathon, walkathon, or cyclothon every single month. It was an ambitious goal, but I was determined to see it through. As I immersed myself in these events, I noticed a vibrant community of cyclists who were passionately engaged in their sport. This observation sparked an idea. What if I could create a record that combined speedcubing and cycling? Not only would it challenge me, but it could also draw attention to speedcubing, a sport I deeply love but that often gets overlooked.

When most people think of speedcubing, they see it as just a toy. I thought the same when I first started. But as I delved deeper into the community and the sport, it pained me to see how little recognition it received. It's not anyone's fault; we tend to only know about sports that receive major media attention.

Determined to change this, I conceived a plan to solve a record number of pyramid-shaped puzzles while riding a bicycle. The challenge was to cycle continuously without touching my feet to the ground and solve puzzles simultaneously. It sounded like a crazy idea, but I believed it could work. When I pitched the idea, they accepted and gave me a target: I needed to solve at least 111 puzzles to set the record.

Planning the attempt was an exercise in precision. I envisioned circling around on my bicycle, receiving scrambled puzzles from a volunteer. I would solve each puzzle as I cycled, then pass the solved puzzle to another volunteer and grab the next scrambled one. The logistics were intricate, but I was confident in my ability to pull it off.

This is the rough chart I had created to explain my ideas to the team that would look after the flow on the day of attempt.

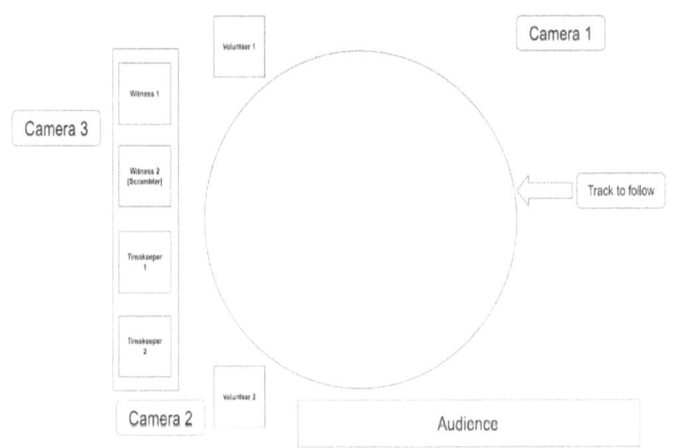

This challenge was more than just about setting a record; it was about raising awareness and recognition for speedcubing in India. It was my way of showing that speedcubing is more than just a pastime; it's a sport that demands skill, concentration, and dedication. And through this endeavor, I hoped to inspire others to see it in the same light.

I practiced diligently for months, upgrading my skills and preparing for my big attempt. I set the date for August 18, 2019, marking it as the day I would combine my passions for speedcubing and cycling in a record-breaking feat. However, as August began, the rain came pouring down relentlessly. It seemed as if the skies had a vendetta against my plans. But I couldn't afford to let the rain hinder my progress. I needed to be ready for the worst-case scenario, which meant practicing in the rain to ensure I wouldn't be thrown off if the weather turned bad on the big day.

Practicing in the rain was grueling. The wet conditions made it easy to slip and fall, and I found myself nursing injuries more often than not. Every fall felt like a setback, but I pushed through, determined to be fully prepared. As the final week before the attempt approached, the heavy rains showed no sign of letting up. I clung to the hope that the rain wouldn't force us to cancel. My team and I brainstormed ways to mitigate the impact of the weather, but given that the attempt was taking place outdoors with no cover, our options were limited.

On the morning of August 18, I woke up to a surprising sight: clear skies and bright sunshine. There was not a drop of rain in sight. It felt like a small miracle.

August 18 turned out to be the first day of the month when it did not rain at all.

August

Sun	Mon	Tue	Wed	Thu	Fri	Sat
				1 +79° night +81°	2 +79° night +79°	3 +77° night +77°
4 +77° night +75°	5 +77° night +77°	6 +79° night +77°	7 +79° night +77°	8 +79° night +79°	9 +79° night +77°	10 +81° night +77°
11 +79° night +77°	12 +81° night +77°	13 +81° night +77°	14 +79° night +77°	15 +81° night +77°	16 +81° night +77°	17 +82° night +77°
18 +82° night +77°	19 +82° night +77°	20 +82° night +77°	21 +81° night +77°	22 +82° night +77°	23 +82° night +77°	24 +82° night +77°
25 +82° night +77°	26 +82° night +77°	27 +82° night +77°	28 +82° night +77°	29 +84° night +77°	30 +81° night +77°	31 +81° night +77°

When you genuinely desire something with all your heart, it's as if the universe conspires to make it happen. I experienced this firsthand on that day. It felt nothing short of miraculous to witness the sky remain clear, with not a drop of rain in sight.

Energized by the favorable weather, I geared up and started the attempt with a sense of optimism. As I cycled and solved puzzles, one after another, I felt a rhythm take over. The target of 111 puzzles soon fell behind me.

I was exhilarated but also determined not to stop there. I set my sights on a new personal goal of 200 puzzles. The sun beat down, and the humidity began to take its toll. My hands grew sweaty, making it increasingly difficult to grip the puzzles. Then, just as I was nearing my new target, a puzzle slipped from my grasp and tumbled to the ground. The attempt had to be halted at that point.

Despite the abrupt end, I had set a new record: 176 puzzles solved while cycling. It was a moment of triumph, not just for me, but for the entire speedcubing community. This achievement was more than a personal milestone; it was a statement. It was a testament to the dedication and skill that speedcubing demands, and a step towards gaining the recognition the sport deserves.

CHAPTER EIGHT

ANTICIPATION

While I was engrossed in preparing for my second World Record attempt, I had no idea that the video of my first record was gaining traction on social media across various countries. It was an incredible and surreal moment when I received an invitation to participate in a talent show in Europe.

Me, on an international talent show? It felt like a dream come true, and I immediately knew I wanted to go.

The process of arranging my participation took several weeks. Forms had to be filled, permissions obtained, and logistics planned. Finally, I found myself on a plane to this new adventure.

Upon arriving at around 12:30 AM, I was greeted by a driver who took me to my hotel. The following day was a free day, which meant no rehearsals or obligations. It was the perfect opportunity to explore the city at my leisure. However, I quickly realized that in order to navigate freely and avoid getting lost, I needed internet access. Without a local SIM card, I was stuck.

The first task was to convert my Euros into the local currency so I could buy a SIM card. I stepped out of my hotel and began asking strangers for directions to a "currency exchange" shop. To my surprise, many people seemed confused. It dawned on me that the language barrier was the culprit, as their local language is the widely spoken language here.

Without internet access to use Google Translate, my attempts at communication were limited. I approached several people, each time hoping they would understand my request. Finally, a kind lady who had overheard my struggles multiple times exclaimed, "Oh! Money changing!" She gave me clear directions, and I followed them eagerly.

I found the currency exchange shop, exchanged my money, and then purchased a new SIM card. With internet access secured, I was ready to explore the vibrant streets. This experience taught me the importance of patience and perseverance, especially when faced with language barriers in a foreign country. It was a small but significant victory that set the tone for my European adventure.

I ventured out to a local grocery shop to pick up the essentials I needed for the week, as well as a few items to take back home. As I roamed the aisles, I found a bottle of water, scanned it with

Google Translate, and confirmed that the word indeed meant water. Satisfied, I decided to take a larger 2.5-liter bottle to ensure I stayed hydrated.

After checking out and returning to my hotel, I eagerly opened the large bottle, ready to quench my thirst. As soon as I twisted the cap, I was met with an unexpected hiss and a burst of fizz. Confused, I took a sip and quickly realized my mistake – I had purchased 2.5 liters of carbonated water instead of still water.

The unexpected surprise was a reminder of the small yet humorous challenges that come with navigating a new country. Despite the initial disappointment, I couldn't help but laugh at the mix-up. It was a small adventure in itself, adding to the tapestry of experiences that made my trip memorable. This little mishap became a story to share and chuckle over, highlighting the unpredictable nature of travel and the lessons learned along the way.

Backstage at the show, I was surrounded by a diverse array of talented individuals from all corners of the globe. The atmosphere was electric, filled with anticipation and excitement. Each contestant had a unique skill or talent they had honed over years. There were dancers, magicians, singers, and performers of every kind, all passionate about their crafts.

One of the participants I met was a bubbleologist. As we talked, we exchanged ideas and stories about our respective passions. She was fascinated by the records I had set, while I was intrigued by the art of creating intricate soap bubbles. Our conversation flowed effortlessly, and it was enlightening to share and learn from someone who had dedicated herself to such a whimsical yet captivating art form.

The experience of being backstage with so many talented individuals was inspiring. It was a reminder of the power of passion and dedication. Each person there had followed their dreams, no matter how unconventional they might seem, and it was a privilege to be among them. My journey to this talent show was not just about showcasing my own talent, but also about connecting with and learning from a global community of performers.

Backstage, surrounded by fellow artists, I was caught off guard when another artist passing by asked, "Hey! You're Indian, right?" For a split second, I braced myself, wondering if a racist comment was coming my way. I nodded cautiously. To my surprise, he continued, "You Indians are so intelligent." Hearing that filled me with pride, realizing how positively people from other countries viewed my homeland.

When my turn came, I felt the weight of the moment. Walking onto the stage, the pressure to perform my best was intense, and nerves started to kick in. Because the show was in their local language, I was given a translating device to help me understand the jury's questions and respond appropriately.

Standing there, I felt immense pride as I introduced myself: "Hello everyone, my name is Chinmay Prabhu, and I have come all the way from India." Representing my country on such a prestigious stage was a dream come true.

The performance began with a glass tank set up on stage. I had specifically requested lukewarm water, considering the chilly weather outside. However, due to some last-minute changes, they couldn't arrange warm water and ended up bringing cold water instead. Despite the mix-up, I went ahead with the performance.

As I submerged myself in the tank, the show commenced. But after solving four puzzles, my fingers started to stiffen from the cold. I could no longer continue. Reluctantly, I got out of the tank, ending my performance faster than expected.

The jury members, who were familiar with my performances, looked shocked. They approached me, clearly puzzled, and asked what had gone wrong. I explained the situation, and they were taken aback. The host then walked over to touch the water, confirming it was indeed cold. The jury and the show's crew were incredibly kind and understanding. They promised to arrange lukewarm water for the next day, offering me another chance to perform.

The following day, as I prepared for my performance, I noticed the crew bringing drums of boiling water onto the stage. My heart sank. I had asked for lukewarm water, not boiling hot! How could I convey this without causing a scene? Is this because of the language barrier that I was facing?

I approached one of the crew members who was pouring the water. Trying to keep the mood light, I joked, "Are you planning to make soup out of me?" He laughed heartily and explained that the boiling water was to balance out with the cold water, reassuring me not to worry. Before my performance, the hosts double-checked the water temperature, ensuring it was just right this time.

With a renewed sense of confidence, I walked up to the jury members and requested them to scramble the puzzles for me. Taking the puzzles with me, I stepped into the tank, ready to give my best performance.

I had a series of scrambled puzzles, much like my World Record attempt. As I started solving them one by one, the audience watched intently. By the end, I had solved seven puzzles, and the crowd erupted in cheers. The jury gave me three yeses, securing my place in the next round. I was elated knowing I would be returning back to this show to continue this incredible journey.

My performance aired on television in 2020. But shortly after, the world was hit by the COVID-19 pandemic, and everything came to a halt. It was a tough time for everyone. The show contacted me to inform me that there would be no further rounds; the pandemic had brought the show to a stop as well.

I felt a pang of sadness, knowing I had lost a significant opportunity. But this disappointment paled in comparison to the global crisis unfolding around us. The pandemic made survival a struggle for many, and my personal loss felt minor in the face of the widespread hardship and uncertainty. It was a reminder that sometimes, the challenges we face are part of a much larger picture, and resilience and empathy become our most valuable strength

CHAPTER NINE

REVIVE

By mid-2021, I was aware of the tough times we were all facing. Despite the challenges, I couldn't escape the persistent feeling that I was doing nothing meaningful. I feared that both I and my beloved sport would fade into obscurity. The question that haunted me was how I could possibly stage a comeback, revive my passion, and leave a mark once more.

I was receiving opportunities, but none of them brought me any joy. One such opportunity came from a regional television show that wanted me to perform my underwater act. I was hopeful, thinking this could be the break I needed.

However, things took a turn for the worse. While one of the crew members was fixing the camera inside the glass tank, the screw was tightened so much that the glass shattered. It felt like a metaphor for my life at that moment. No matter what I tried, things seemed to go wrong from the very start.

It was disheartening. Every attempt felt like a step backward, and I couldn't shake the feeling that I was stuck in a cycle of failure. My confidence wavered as each setback seemed to confirm my growing doubts. It was a tough time, and I struggled to find the motivation to keep pushing forward.

One night, as I was watching a movie, a skydiving scene flickered on the screen. The adrenaline, the sheer thrill of the freefall, caught my imagination. An audacious thought struck me: what if I could solve a puzzle while skydiving? At first, I dismissed it as a fleeting fancy, a wild notion not meant to be taken seriously. But as the days passed, the idea stayed with me, refusing to be silenced.

Unable to ignore the persistent thought, I finally picked up the phone and called a skydiving institute. My excitement was quickly deflated when the first two places rejected my idea outright, not even bothering to explain why it was impossible. Undeterred, I made a third call, hoping for different responses.

The man on the other end of the line listened patiently before speaking. "Imagine you're driving a car at around 200 kilometers per hour," he began. "Now, roll down the window and stick your hand out. The wind would push your hand back, right? Now you're telling me you want to solve a puzzle at that speed? The pieces would slip out of your hand, and there's a real risk of someone getting hurt."

His explanation was blunt and sobering, yet it only fueled my determination. I knew the idea was crazy, but I couldn't shake the feeling that it was exactly the kind of challenge I needed to break free from my inertia. The question was no longer whether it was possible, but how I could make it happen safely. This was my shot at reclaiming my passion and making a memorable comeback.

Nobody in India was willing to entertain my idea. Every skydiving institute I approached turned me down, but I didn't let their rejections deter me.

I had already begun practicing at home. Yes, you read that right—at home.

Determined to prepare myself, I grabbed a chair and started mimicking the skydiving position I had seen online. Balancing my body on the chair, I tried to imagine the force of the wind against me as I worked to solve the puzzle. It was a makeshift setup, but it was the best I could do under the circumstances.

I had realized that my dream, however unconventional, had the power to shape my reality. If I wanted this badly enough, I could make it happen. It was all about believing in the impossible and turning it into something real. Every day, I practiced with unwavering dedication.

My living room became my training ground, where I battled imaginary winds and perfected my puzzle-solving skills. I embraced the power of my dreams, knowing that they had the potential to transform my reality.

After numerous attempts, I finally found someone who believed my idea was possible. This person agreed to help me make my dream a reality. However, the next hurdle was a daunting one: raising the substantial amount of money required. Skydives are expensive, and I would need multiple practice jumps to acclimate to the intense wind conditions. To add to the pressure, I was required to make an upfront payment.

Realizing that raising such a large sum would be no easy feat, I decided to turn to crowdfunding. I began posting about my campaign on all my social media platforms, urging my followers to support me. I spammed direct messages to everyone I knew, swallowing my pride because I knew this was the only way to achieve my goal. I had no shame—this had to be done if I was to earn the title.

As the funds started to trickle in, I encountered a new set of challenges. I had received a target to solve the puzzle within 30 seconds during freefall. The evidence required was extensive, not only documenting my attempt but also including verification of the skydiver who would accompany me on the tandem jump. Every detail had to be properly recorded and verified.

The most daunting guideline, however, was that I wasn't allowed to jump with the puzzle in my hand. Instead, it had to be handed to me mid-air after the jump. This added an extra layer of complexity to an already formidable task. But I was undeterred. Each new obstacle only fueled my determination to succeed.

Even though I desperately wanted to set my records on Indian soil, nothing seemed to be going in my favor. No place was willing to provide a skydiver to film the attempt mid-air. Determined not to give up, I reached out to skydiving institutes in multiple countries. Each response was a rejection, with different reasons why my idea was unfeasible.

But then, something magical happened during a call with a skydiving institute. They listened to my proposal and explained why it wouldn't work there—they conducted their jumps over land, and if the puzzle slipped from my hand, it could cause serious injury to someone below. Of course, I didn't want that to happen. But instead of a flat-out rejection, they offered a glimmer of hope. They suggested I pitch my idea to a skydiving center in Chonburi, where jumps took place over water bodies. In the worst-case scenario, if the puzzle slipped from my hand, it would fall harmlessly into the water.

Without wasting a moment, I called the Chonburi institute. I explained my idea in detail, laying out the plan and the precautions. To my immense relief, they said they were on board. They were willing to make it happen. I wanted to make sure they understood what I meant and there was no confusion due to a language barrier. They confirmed sending me a message that it was possible.

I could hardly believe it. My dream was finally coming to life. The excitement was overwhelming—this was it, the moment I had been waiting for. All the rejections and hurdles had led me to this point, and now, we were good to go. It was really happening.

CHAPTER TEN

EUPHORIA

With my next attempt scheduled in another country, I needed better funding. As I reached out to various potential sponsors, I was contacted by a well-known firm. They were organizing an event in Goa for their employees and wanted me to perform as a motivational speaker.

"Me? A motivational speaker?" I asked in disbelief. "I've never done anything like that before."

The representative reassured me. "We find your story exciting and aligned with our goals. We want you to share your journey and teach our employees how to solve a pyramid-shaped puzzle. Use it to illustrate how they can achieve anything they set their minds to if they're curious and willing enough."

The fee they offered would be helpful to fund my skydiving record attempt. I agreed and immediately started working on my script. The event was set for April 4th, so I had little time to prepare.

I arrived at the hotel on April 3rd and had a rehearsal talk with the team. By late afternoon, I was free for the rest of the day. I had an idea before leaving for Goa: I wanted to go bungee jumping at a nearby site. With my first skydive attempt scheduled for April 14th, I thought experiencing the sensation of freefalling would be invaluable.

I headed to the bungee jump site with an audacious plan in mind. I intended to attempt the jump and follow similar guidelines that of skydiving, as a precursor to my skydiving attempt. After explaining my idea to the management at the site, they were eager to facilitate the attempt.

As I signed the consent form, a wave of fear washed over me. The form clearly stated that they wouldn't be responsible if anything happened to me. My anxiety stemmed not just from the inherent danger, but also from the fact that I hadn't informed anyone—neither my family nor my friends—about where I was or what I was about to do.

Standing on the edge, waiting for the signal to jump, my heart pounded in my chest.

The instructor's countdown echoed in my ears, and with a deep breath, I launched myself forward, clutching a box containing a scrambled Pyraminx puzzle. The world flipped upside down as I descended, and I quickly opened the box. One of the witnesses started the stopwatch, marking the beginning of the attempt.

The sensation of freefalling was both terrifying and exhilarating. My heart raced as I moved my hands faster than ever, solving the puzzle. Within 7.90 seconds, the Pyraminx was complete, and I let out a triumphant scream to signal the end of my attempt.

The thrill of falling at such speed was intense, yet I found myself wanting to experience it again. As I reached the ground, the crew handed me the footage from multiple angles, capturing every moment of the attempt. I felt a rush of euphoria and disbelief as I called home, laughing uncontrollably while recounting the surreal experience.

I returned back to the hotel, ready to deliver a powerful performance as a motivational speaker. The success had filled me with newfound confidence and energy. I was eager to share my story and inspire the audience with the message that with curiosity and determination, anything is possible.

The very next day, I gave my first talk to the corporate group, and it went absolutely amazing. Standing in front of an audience, sharing my journey and the lessons I had learned, was an exhilarating experience. As I spoke, I realized just how much I had to share that could inspire others to pursue their passions—whether it was playing a sport, collecting coins, or anything else they loved.

The audience's reactions were incredible. They were engaged, nodding along, and asking thoughtful questions. It was at that moment that I understood the power of my story. It wasn't just about my achievements; it was about the journey, the struggles, and the persistence to keep going despite setbacks.

I felt a deep sense of fulfillment knowing that my experiences could motivate someone to keep doing what they love. It was a revelation that opened up new possibilities for me—sharing my story, inspiring others, and encouraging them to follow their passion, no matter how unconventional it might seem at the beginning.

As I returned home after the exhilarating talk, my mind buzzed with newfound confidence for the skydive. The sensation of freefall had captivated me completely—I had tasted the thrill of descending through the sky, and it left me craving more.

I sent the evidence from my bungee jump ahead too because nobody I know of, had solved a puzzle in the manner I did. Also the guidelines were well followed. The footage was reviewed and evidence was checked. It was stated as an official world record for the title "Fastest to solve a rotating puzzle tetrahedron upside down". The bungee jump record felt like a gift from the universe.

Now, with determination fueling my every move, I delved into the process of securing my visa and completing the necessary documents. Emerging from the shadow of the pandemic's end, each form and requirement became a stepping stone towards realizing my dream of soaring through the skies.

CHAPTER ELEVEN

LEAP

I arrived in Thailand in the early hours of April 13th, sleepy but excited. A car took me away to my hotel in Pattaya, where I immediately underwent a COVID-19 RT-PCR test. It was 7 a.m. when the swab was taken, and I was informed that the results would be available between 11 a.m. to 3 p.m. Until then, I had to remain in quarantine. That meant I could not leave my room until I got back negative results.

The hours dragged on. I called the reception multiple times, but each time, I received the same answer: "Not yet." As the clock inched towards midnight, my anxiety grew. I had a skydive attempt scheduled for the next day, and without my test results, I couldn't step out of my room. My mind raced with worry. What if they were not informing me because the results were positive? What if I had to cancel my skydive? thoughts started to clutter in my head.

Finally, at 11:50 p.m., I decided to make one last call. If I didn't get an answer, I'd cancel the attempt. The manager picked up, and when I asked about the results, he said, "Yes, the reports are ready. It's negative. You're free to go."

Relief washed over me. After hours of uncertainty and overthinking, I was finally free to step out of my room and proceed with my plans. The weight lifted off my shoulders as I prepared for the adventure that awaited me the next day.

A van arrived outside my hotel to pick me up for the skydive attempt. As I climbed in, my nerves were palpable. Upon reaching the site, I explained how the cube needed to be passed mid-air. To my shock, I was informed at the reception that no objects were allowed to be carried during the jump. My jaw dropped. I had received confirmation beforehand, invested all my money, and now this? I couldn't leave without attempting it. Panicking, I showed them the WhatsApp chat where I had confirmed this multiple times. They asked me to wait.

My anxiety peaked as I waited, fearing this might turn into a colossal mess. Eventually, they returned with the news: the instructors were aware of the attempt, and we could proceed with the attempt.

Finally, it was a green light. I was led to a waiting room where they explained how to maintain the banana pose mid-air. My heart raced as I tried to absorb the instructions. We were waiting for about 3 hours for the sky to become clear.

When the time came, a big smile spread across my face as I walked toward the aircraft. The puzzle, scrambled according to World Cube Association guidelines, was packed in a box and sealed with duct tape.

Inside the aircraft, we ascended to 13,000 feet. The air was noticeably colder. When the door opened and I saw skydivers jumping out, it felt surreal—like a scene straight out of a movie. Then it was our turn. The thought of falling out of the aircraft made me a little scared. My instructor and I stood on the edge of the aircraft, and the cameraman, who would film mid-air, carried the cube to pass it to me. I was told that the cameraman would jump and we would jump right after him.

I saw him jump, and my instructor tapped on my shoulder indicating it was time. I took a leap, and assumed the banana pose as instructed. The cameraman approached mid-air, attempting to pass me the cube, but I missed it.

Not once, but twice. For the attempt to be successful, the puzzle had to be completely solved during freefall. Solving the puzzle after the parachute opened was not allowed. I was losing precious freefall time. On the third attempt, I lunged aggressively and grabbed the cube.

Solving it mid-air was a challenge. I had to hold the puzzle in a way that prevented it from flying out of my hand. Thanks to my practice, I managed, but the triangular shape of the puzzle caused it to spin in the strong winds, scrambling further. I held on tightly, ensuring no pieces moved unless I intended them to. This impacted my speed, but I persevered.

Just before the parachute opened, I completed the puzzle, though we were unsure of the time it had taken. According to the guidelines, it had to be done in under 30 seconds.

Once I landed, I started celebrating, elated to have solved the puzzle in freefall on my first skydive attempt, even without knowing if it was a record.

The footage was checked, revealing it took me 24.22 seconds. That was it—a new World Record was set. History was made. I wanted to set this record on Indian soil but due to some uncontrollable factors that couldn't be possible. So I took India along with me. I pulled out the flag I had brought along and posed triumphantly outside the aircraft.

This all felt like a part of God's plan, and it was like a dream come true.

The news of this record broke in the media from across the world. Reactions started to pour in. Everyone was shocked to witness what had just taken place.

This achievement is dedicated to every one of you who supported me, whether directly or indirectly. I know I might have bombarded you with crowdfunding links as I pursued this dream, and I'm deeply grateful for your patience and generosity. This record wouldn't have been possible without your willingness to share my cause or assist me in managing my finances. Your support has been invaluable, and I thank you from the bottom of my heart.

When I first envisioned breaking this record, it seemed like an impossible dream. The road was filled with challenges and uncertainties, but knowing that I had a community of supporters behind me made all the difference. Each share, each donation, and each word of encouragement fueled my determination to push through the toughest moments.

To my family, friends, and even strangers who believed in me enough to contribute in any way—they say it takes a village, and you all were my village. You helped transform a solitary dream into a shared victory, and for that, I am eternally grateful.

In every twist and turn of this journey, your support reminded me of the power of community and the incredible things we can achieve together. This record is not just mine; it's collective effort, faith, and generosity of everyone who played a part. Thank you for helping me turn this dream into reality.

CHAPTER TWELVE

CREATIVITY

Once, I was traveling to Shirdi with my parents. Amidst my plans, I wasn't certain if I'd have the time to visit the popular devotional theme park there. I noticed that their social media account was quite active, so I decided to drop them a message, asking if it was necessary to buy tickets in advance or if I could get them at the park. I was particularly concerned about the closing time of the ticket counters.

When I eventually visited the theme park, a staff member approached me, mentioning that he had seen my social media profile and was impressed by the cube mosaic artworks I had posted in the past. Intrigued by my work, he asked if we could set something up in the park that could potentially lead to setting a new record.

After returning home, I began to delve into the logistics. I calculated the dimensions needed to set a record, the number of cubes required, and various other details. Initially, I envisioned a temporary artwork for the record, something that would be displayed for a few days and then dismantled. However, the park had different plans. They wanted a permanent installation, a piece of art that would stand the test of time. The prospect thrilled me. The idea of having a permanent artwork that I could revisit in the future was immensely exciting.

I initially pitched an artwork using 500 cubes. After several discussions and revisions, the plan evolved. We decided to create a masterpiece using more than 4,000 cubes. This was, by far, the largest artwork I had ever attempted.

Realizing the enormity of the project, I knew I needed help. Guess who came to my rescue? My college friend, the same one who used to drop me off at the swimming pool for practice sessions. We decided that I would lead the project while he assisted with quality checks and assembly.

A month later, we went to the theme park, eagerly awaiting the arrival of the cubes. None of us had seen what 4,000 cubes looked like together. To our astonishment, a full-sized truck pulled up, unloading 11 enormous boxes. Seeing those boxes, I felt a mix of excitement and fear.

The puzzles arrived around 6 PM, and by 7 PM, we were already at work. The project had officially begun. We organized the cubes on tables, numbering them perfectly to ensure each block went to its designated spot.

For four straight days, I worked 16 hours a day. I don't know where I found the energy to sustain such a grueling schedule. It felt as though a higher power was guiding me, fueling my determination.

The artwork, an impressive creation made from 4,212 cubes, earned a place in the India Book of Records. This remarkable feat not only showcases the creativity and dedication involved but also highlights the skill and perseverance required to achieve such a significant milestone. The size of the artwork is 10ft x 15ft.

Reflecting back now, I realize how improbable it was to complete such a massive project so swiftly. Yet, we did it. The sense of accomplishment and the joy of seeing the finished artwork made every moment worth it.

Now, whenever I visit that place, I can relive those incredible memories, marveling at the permanent testament to our hard work and passion.

CHAPTER THIRTEEN

UNBROKEN

It was nearly five years ago, in October 2019, when I found myself backstage at the talent show in Europe, waiting for my turn to perform. Amidst the nerves and excitement, I met someone who would add a fascinating twist to my journey, a bubbleologist from Moldova. She was an artist in her own right, creating mesmerizing, gigantic bubbles that seemed to float in slow motion, capturing the light and leaving everyone in awe.

As we struck up a conversation, she learned about my own story of setting 2 World Records. Her eyes lit up with curiosity and excitement, eager to understand the process of setting a world record. She shared her dream of one day achieving such a feat herself. On the other side, I found myself captivated by her craft, eager to learn the art of making those magnificent bubbles.

Our connection didn't end when the cameras stopped rolling. We kept in touch long after the show, our conversations a blend of dreams and techniques. She guided me through the intricacies of bubble making via video calls, explaining the delicate balance of ingredients and the subtle techniques needed to create the perfect bubble. In return, I offered her advice and strategies for planning and attempting a world record.

The first time I attempted to create a big bubble, it burst almost instantly. Frustrated but hopeful, I realized that the solution I used needed to be perfectly balanced and tailored to Mumbai's weather conditions. With her guidance and my persistence, I kept experimenting, each attempt bringing me closer to mastering this delicate art. I practiced for weeks, but due to other ongoing activities I stopped paying attention to the idea of solving a puzzle inside a soap bubble and the thought completely left my mind.

One fine day, I got a message from her, stating after multiple attempts she had finally managed to set a World Record title in her name, and her accomplishment sparked a fire within me. Inspired by her success, I decided to take my own challenge more seriously. My goal was to solve the Pyraminx puzzle inside a soap bubble without bursting it. I sent this idea ahead and, after a waiting period, received a set of guidelines for the attempt.

Before the guidelines arrived, I already started practicing as I was invited to participate in a local talent show. I thought, what better opportunity to test my idea in front of a live audience? On the day of the performance, with nerves and excitement coursing through me, I kept trying multiple times and the bubble kept bursting and after about 4 bubble bursts, I managed to solve the puzzle inside the bubble in roughly 50 seconds. Once the puzzle was solved, the next challenge was sliding my hands out with the bubble staying intact. The audience had never witnessed anything like it before; their astonished faces fueled my determination even further. I was the only person in the world to have solved a puzzle inside a soap bubble without bursting it.

After a few weeks, the official guidelines were received, they were different from what I had attempted at the talent show. But that was okay; my primary goal at the show was to prove to myself and the audience that it was possible, not to set the record just yet.

I attempted the record two more times after receiving the guidelines, but both attempts ended in failure. Even the slightest movement in the air would result in bursting of the bubble. The movement in the air could be because of people walking nearby, people clapping, or my hands getting dry too quick. It seemed impossible to figure out how to keep the bubble intact while solving the puzzle. I immersed myself in research, studying the intricate details of how multiple different factors affect the soap bubbles.

Years passed since I first conceived the idea. By now I had already attempted the record thrice following the guideline but it always ended in failure. In February 2024, I was ready to try again for the fourth time.

The atmosphere was tense as I began the attempt. I carefully uncovered the puzzle and dipped it into the bubble solution. The timer began right when the puzzle was uncovered. I blew up a bubble on the table and gently pushed the puzzle inside. I dipped both my hands in the solution, and then I slowly inserted them into the bubble and began solving the puzzle with minimal movements.

Getting a good grip on the puzzle was next to impossible as the puzzle and my hands were soaked in bubble water. It would slip out of my hands easily.

Every second felt like an eternity, but my focus remained unbroken. Finally, I did it, the puzzle was solved and I slowly slid my hands out hoping the bubble would not burst. Once my hands were out I gave a clear stop signal to alert the witnesses that the attempt was over and the timer needed to be stopped.

The feat was achieved in 32.69 seconds. The feeling of accomplishment was indescribable. After years of practice, failures, and learning, I had set my fifth world record title.

Achieving this particular record was the most challenging feat I've ever attempted. In most of my previous records, I had some degree of control over the variables involved. However, this particular challenge involved a delicate bubble that could burst at the slightest touch, making it incredibly unpredictable and difficult to manage. The experience tested my patience like never before.

CHAPTER FOURTEEN

COURAGE

During my journey of setting records, some of my reels went viral on Instagram. It wasn't all applause and praise, though. While many people celebrated my achievements, I also faced a fair share of trolling. The criticism and negative comments didn't just fade away; I still encounter online trolls to this very day.

This past decade hasn't been easy on my mind. Ever since I set my first record, I've faced relentless trolling on social media. The spectrum of negativity has been wide, ranging from body shaming to outright abusive comments during my Instagram live sessions. What hurt the most was that most of these trolls were from my own country—India. It was disheartening to witness such hostility from my own people.

In today's world, we see toxic trolls being rewarded with likes and validation from others. Those of us who strive to create something from nothing are often reduced to mere jokes in the eyes of society. It's a harsh reality, but it's one I've come to accept.

And try thinking from a different perspective. Who are these trolls, really? They are people like you and me, but without the courage to live the lives they desire. They hide behind their screens, lashing out at those who dare to chase their dreams. If only they could give their own dreams a chance, without fear of judgment, who knows what they might achieve? They might actually start living, truly living, for the first time.

Despite the negativity, I remind myself that there will always be countless reasons to stop doing what you love. The criticisms, the mockery, the doubt—they all pile up, creating a mountain of excuses. But amidst this mountain, there's always one reason to keep going. And that reason is the most important one: because you're alive. You're living in a world where magic happens, where dreams can come true if you have the courage to pursue them.

So, I choose to focus on that one reason to keep going. I choose to live, to dream, and to create, despite the trolls. Because in the end, the magic of life lies in our ability to rise above the negativity and to keep pushing forward, no matter what.

If you find yourself holding back due to the fear of being judged or trolled, please don't let it stop you. Be free. Be happy.

I have started to draw inspiration from some content creators who have turned trolling into their advantage. They have made it their selling point, putting out content specifically to invite trolls, and it works wonders for their marketing. They've found a way to turn negativity into something positive.

Now that trolling has been addressed, I want you to think back to when you were a child or even now as an adult. What is that one thing that made you feel truly alive? The one thing that made time seem to fly by without you even noticing? It could be anything—reading books, coloring, cooking your favorite meal, or binge-watching your favorite show. When was the last time you did this without having other thoughts in your head?

You've probably heard the saying that no matter what happens, you should always keep your inner child alive. But what does that really mean? What is the inner child? What's different between you now and the child you once were?

The inner child is that part of you that engages in activities purely out of love and joy, without the stress and worries that come with adult life. It's about finding and doing what you love, simply because it makes you happy.

When you reconnect with that inner child, you begin to see the world with fresh eyes. You realize that the pressures and judgments of adulthood often cloud the simple pleasures that once brought you immense joy. Embracing your inner child is not about escaping responsibilities but about finding balance—allowing yourself to indulge in moments of pure, unadulterated happiness. It's about giving yourself permission to be playful, to explore, and to dream without the weight of societal expectations. So, take a moment to reflect on what ignites your passion and make time for it. In doing so, you'll discover that life becomes richer and more fulfilling, and you'll find the strength to rise above the negativity and continue pursuing your dreams with renewed energy.

CHAPTER FIFTEEN

GOAL

Throughout my journey, I've found that asking myself four key questions has been instrumental in achieving my goals. Whether I'm aiming for a world record or tackling a daily task, these questions have a way of turning aspirations into reality. I'm not trying to impose this on you, but as a friendly piece of advice. If you're setting a goal, consider asking yourself these questions. I genuinely believe that doing so can significantly increase your chances of success.

Each goal, big or small, benefits from a moment of reflection and clarity. These questions serve as a guide, helping to break down the path to achievement into manageable steps. They force you to think deeply about your motivations, resources, and strategies, ensuring that your goals are not just dreams but actionable plans. By integrating this practice into your routine, you'll find that the road to success becomes clearer and more attainable, turning obstacles into stepping stones.

1. Is it Specific?

Setting a specific goal means being crystal clear about what you want to achieve. For instance, saying "Running a marathon" is quite broad and doesn't give you a clear path forward. On the other hand, saying "Running 10 kilometers in The Mumbai Marathon 2025" is much more specific.

It not only defines the distance but also sets the event and year, providing a clear target to aim for. Specific goals like these give you a roadmap and make it easier to plan your training, nutrition, and overall preparation. They bring clarity to your ambitions and help you stay focused on what needs to be done to succeed.

With a clear goal in mind, you're more likely to stay motivated and track your progress effectively. Plus, achieving these specific milestones boosts your confidence, encouraging you to set and conquer even bigger challenges.

2. Is it Measurable?

Measuring progress is key to achieving your goals effectively. When a goal is measurable, you can track your advancements and see exactly how close you are to reaching it. Including specific numbers or metrics makes this tracking straightforward. For example, saying "Solving the puzzle in under 10 seconds" or "Increasing profits by at least 15% by the end of December" gives you clear benchmarks to aim for. This way, you can monitor your performance over time, adjust your strategies if needed, and celebrate milestones along the way. Measurable goals not only keep you focused but also provide a sense of accomplishment as you see your efforts paying off. It also boosts your motivation by showing tangible results of your hard work and dedication. Remember, the clearer your metrics, the easier it will be to stay on track and make informed decisions about your next steps.

3. Is it Achievable?

Setting goals that are challenging yet achievable is all about finding that sweet spot where you're pushing yourself to grow without overwhelming yourself. It's crucial to consider your current resources, skills, and the time you have available. This evaluation helps in setting realistic goals that you can work towards with confidence.

For instance, if your aim is to run a marathon, it's essential to break down the process into manageable steps. Start by setting smaller goals, like running a certain distance each week or improving your pace gradually. This approach not only builds your stamina and endurance over time but also boosts your confidence as you achieve these milestones.

Moreover, setting achievable goals prevents burnout and maintains motivation. It allows you to focus on making consistent progress rather than feeling pressured to achieve an unrealistic target.

4. Can Timeline be set?

Setting deadlines or timelines for your hobbies is like giving yourself a roadmap with clear checkpoints. It adds a sense of urgency and helps you prioritize activities effectively. For example, setting a goal like "finish knitting a sweater by the end of November" or "learn to play three new songs on the guitar by the end of August" sets specific timeframes for achieving these milestones.

Having a deadline encourages commitment because it gives you a target to work towards. It's like planning a fun adventure—you set a date for when you want to accomplish something, which motivates you to stay dedicated and make consistent progress. This timeframe also holds you accountable, allowing you to track your achievements and adjust your schedule if necessary to stay on track with your hobby goals. Ultimately, it ensures you make progress.

Epilogue

What does this book mean to me? Is it the culmination of my journey in speedcubing, marking the end of an era? Far from it. It's actually just the beginning of something even more extraordinary. From today onward, I feel a sense of companionship—we're in this together, each of us chasing our dreams.

I've never been one to plan too much for the future. It's always been like taking a shot in the dark, following my instincts and passions wherever they lead. And you know what? That unpredictability excites me. It's the thrill of the unknown, the potential for new discoveries and adventures that keeps me going.

Whatever lies ahead, I'm certain of one thing: I'll be happy. Whether my next endeavors succeed or fail, I'll embrace it all because that's the essence of life. The universe operates in mysterious ways, and sometimes, we have to stumble and fall countless times before we find our footing. It's in those moments of struggle that success emerges.

After reflecting on my journey and sharing my story, I invite you to embark on your own path of discovery and growth. Whether it's picking up a new hobby, setting a challenging goal, or nurturing a long-held dream, now is the perfect time to take that first step. Embrace the thrill of learning something new or mastering a skill you've always admired. It's in the pursuit of these passions that we find fulfillment and purpose.

Setting a goal gives you something to strive for—a compass guiding your efforts and measuring your progress. Whether it's running a marathon, learning a new language, or creating art, each milestone achieved brings a sense of accomplishment that fuels your journey further. Don't hesitate to dream big and push beyond your comfort zone. The challenges you face along the way only serve to strengthen your resolve and shape your character.

Remember, every journey is unique, and setbacks are part of the adventure. Embrace them as opportunities for growth and learning. Just as I've learned from my failures and triumphs in speedcubing, your journey will be enriched by the experiences gained along the way. Stay resilient, stay curious, and stay committed to your aspirations.

Above all, find joy in the process. Cherish the moments of discovery, celebrate your achievements, and find inspiration in the pursuit of your passions. By nurturing your dreams with dedication and love, you'll not only enrich your own life but also inspire those around you. So, take that leap, set your sights high, and embrace the journey ahead.

Together, let's make each day a step towards achieving our dreams, crafting a life filled with purpose and fulfillment.